Lewis and Clark: Into the Wilderness

written by Daniel Rosen
illustrated by Ron Himler

**McGraw-Hill
School Division**

New York   Farmington

In 1804, a brave band of explorers led by Meriwether Lewis and William Clark set off from St. Louis and traveled up the Missouri River on a two-and-a-half year voyage. The explorers traveled into the strange, uncharted wilderness and trekked thousands of miles to the Pacific Ocean. Their trip, which changed the United States forever, remains one of the great stories of American history.

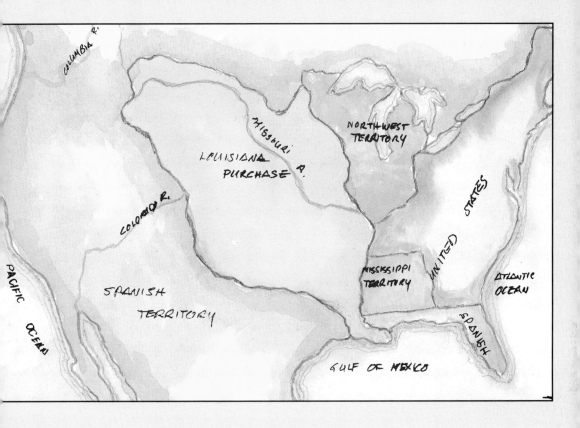

The story begins in 1803, when the United States was a nation of five million people that stretched only from the Atlantic Ocean to the Mississippi River. President Thomas Jefferson bought an enormous parcel of land from Napoleon Bonaparte, the leader of France. *The Louisiana Purchase*, as it was called, doubled the size of the United States and stretched the new nation's borders all the way to what is now the state of Idaho.

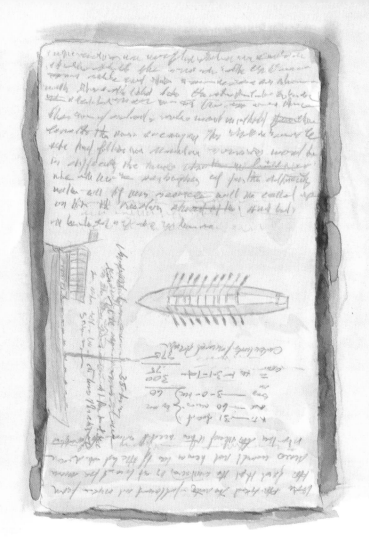

President Jefferson decided to send a group of soldiers to explore the new addition to the United States. To lead the group, he chose his personal secretary Meriwether Lewis, a soldier and experienced woodsman.

To prepare for the trip, Jefferson sent Lewis to meet and learn from the best scientists in America. Lewis immersed himself in an intense study of medicine, navigation, botany, and various other environmental sciences.

Lewis realized that the complex nature of his mission required a co-leader who was both completely trustworthy and a skilled frontiersman. He turned to his friend William Clark, his former commander during his days in the militia. Lewis named Clark his co-captain.

Together, they assembled a crew of about 40 men for their trip, naming their history-making group the *Corps of Discovery*. An especially noteworthy member of the Corps was Lewis's huge Newfoundland dog, Seaman. He helped with guarding the camps, hunting, and was an expert at retrieving submerged game birds from the river after the soldiers shot them. Lewis's close and constant companion, Seaman survived the whole treacherous journey—including several attempts to steal him!

Lewis and Clark spent the winter of 1804 getting ready for the trip. Lewis was responsible for buying supplies for the journey. Thanks to his excellent record-keeping, we know exactly what he bought: 150 yards of cloth to make into tents, 10 pounds of fish hooks, 12 pounds of soap, and 193 pounds of dried beef and vegetable soup.

On May 14, 1804, they loaded up their big keelboat and smaller canoe-like boats, called *pirogues*, and left St. Louis heading up the Missouri River.

It is difficult to comprehend today what it was like for these hardy explorers to set off into a remote wilderness about which so little was known. Lewis and Clark had no idea how far they would have to travel to get to the Pacific, no idea of the height of the Rocky Mountains they would have to cross—or what lay beyond them.

Near what is now Pierre, South Dakota, the Corps of Discovery had their worst encounter with Native Americans. Unlike most other tribes, the Teton Sioux did not want to cooperate with the explorers; they were insulted by the glass beads and trinkets Lewis offered in exchange for their help. The Teton Sioux chiefs demanded boats and guns before they would allow the Americans to continue up the Missouri River.

In a dramatic showdown, a warrior grabbed the bow line of one of the boats. Lewis and Clark ordered the men to battle stations. On the boats, the Corps of Discovery remained steadfast, ready to fire, while on shore hundreds of Teton Sioux stood poised with arrows in their bows. Fortunately, a Sioux chief named Black Buffalo stepped in and ordered the warriors to let Lewis and Clark continue their journey.

Lewis and Clark both kept daily journals, and Clark was responsible for mapping the journey. The maps that he drew proved to be amazingly accurate.

As the Corps of Discovery progressed farther into the wild, Lewis recorded information about the many plants and animals he had never seen before.

Here is an excerpt from Lewis's journal, in September 1804:

"Having for many days past confined myself to the boat, I determined to devote this day to amuse myself on shore with my gun and view . . . the country. . . . This scenery already rich pleasing and beautiful was still farther heightened by immense herds of Buffalo, deer Elk and Antelopes which we saw in every direction feeding on the hills and plains."

Lewis marveled over coyotes, antelopes, gray wolves and, most of all, the fierce mountain grizzly bears. Native Americans had warned Lewis about the size and strength of the grizzly bears, but Lewis was convinced that their rifles would protect them from the bears.

One day, Lewis and another soldier were out hunting and were attacked by a grizzly. Both men fired at the charging bear and both hit it. The bear fell, but as the soldiers approached, much to their surprise, the huge grizzly rose to its feet and charged again! Fortunately, Lewis and his friend had already reloaded their single-shot muskets, and with another round of fire, they brought the mighty bear down. Never again did Lewis underestimate the mighty grizzly bear!

In late October the Corps reached a village of the friendly
Mandan tribe. The co-captains decided to build their winter quarters
there, and during that time, met someone who would become one of
the most important members of the Corps of Discovery.

Sacajawea, a member of the Shoshone people, had been captured
by the Hidatsa as a young girl but now lived among the Mandan
with her husband, Toussaint Charbonneau, a French trapper
and trader.

Sacajawea explained to the captains how she could help them.
She knew the Western territory from her childhood and also knew
that Lewis and Clark planned to buy horses from the Shoshone for
their passage across the Rocky Mountains. The captains saw the
value of Sacajawea's knowledge and hired her and Charbonneau
as guides.

By April, the Corps of Discovery, along with Sacajawea, her husband, and their two-month old baby boy, was ready to continue west.

The Great Falls on the Missouri River proved to be a difficult portage, and by July the Corps was already lagging behind schedule; they needed to hurry so that they could cross over the Rocky Mountains before the snows of early autumn. Then, to make matters worse, they couldn't find the Shoshone from whom they needed to buy horses.

Finally in August they met with a group of Shoshone. Much to Sacajawea's delight, the chief was her brother whom she hadn't seen in many years. Sacajawea told her brother to sell the Corps the horses they needed; Clark wrote in his journal that without Sacajawea, the Shoshone traders would never have sold them the horses, and the Corps might have had to turn back.

With their newly purchased horses, the Corps of Discovery
began the dangerous passage through the Rocky Mountains. It was
late in the season, and as they climbed, the weather turned bitterly
cold, with snow steadily accumulating. These were the darkest days
of the trip—the explorers were exhausted from walking through the
deep snow on dangerous, narrow trails. They were low on food, but
they realized that to quit would mean certain death. With great
courage and endurance, they pressed on.

In November they finally emerged from the mountains. A war
party of Nez Percé immediately confronted the weary travelers. It
was another tense moment, but when the Nez Percé saw Sacajawea
and her baby, they knew the travelers were peaceful—no war party
would travel with a woman and a baby. The Nez Percé put down
their weapons and provided food and shelter for the
Corps of Discovery.

On the Missouri River, the men had been fighting their way
upstream. After the Rockies, on the westerly flowing Snake and
Columbia Rivers, they were going downstream. Within a few weeks
they were in view of the Pacific Ocean. In his journal of November 7,
Clark wrote: *"Ocean in view...oh the joy!"* The Corps of Discovery
had traveled over 4,100 miles.

The Corps of Discovery spent the winter of 1805-6 with the Clatsop at the mouth of the Columbia River, near present-day, Astoria, Oregon.

The return trip east was much easier, since they now were familiar with the terrain. Once across the Rockies, the trip downstream on the Missouri was a comparative vacation—while heading upstream, a good day's hard paddling had gained them only 20 miles, but moving downstream, with easy paddling, they averaged 70 miles a day.

Arriving in St. Louis, the men were treated like conquering heroes. Lewis and Clark then proceeded to Washington, where they were greeted by President Jefferson. Lewis and Clark conferred with Jefferson, showing him their maps and sharing all the information they had gained from their expedition.

What did Lewis and Clark accomplish? They explored and mapped the new territory, travelling more than 8,000 miles to bring back new plants and animals that had never before been seen by Americans in the east. They created maps of the new territory for the trappers, traders, and settlers who were soon to come, and their newly acquired knowledge of the land served to support the United States' claim to the Pacific Northwest when boundary disputes arose with Great Britain in the 1840s.

Even in those early days, Lewis and Clark were regarded as great heroes—the Corps of Discovery captured the spirit of adventure shared by many in the new nation.

Today, nearly 200 years later, in modern, industrial America, the remarkable story of Lewis and Clark and the Corps of Discovery still captures the imagination of Americans. Every year, adventurous people follow the path of Lewis and Clark to see the country, the rivers, mountains, and rock formations, on paths traced by the Corps of Discovery. They hope to recapture some of the courage of the brave band of explorers who ventured into a land unknown to them, the courage that gave them strength, and helped them survive the dangerous journey, and the spirit that brought the travelers back, full of tales of a wondrous, new America.